ON A CLEAR DAY

An Artist's Perspective On Energy Healing

Illustrations by the Author

An iregina Chronicle

Balboa Press books may be ordered through booksellers or by contacting:

Balboa Press
A Division of Hay House
1663 Liberty Drive
Bloomington, IN 47403
www.balboapress.com
1 (877) 407-4847

Interior Image Credit: iregina

ISBN: 978-1-9822-3371-6 (sc)
ISBN: 978-1-9822-3372-3 (e)

Library of Congress Control Number: 2019912658

Print information available on the last page.

Balboa Press rev. date: 01/24/2020

BALBOA
PRESS
A DIVISION OF HAY HOUSE

Acknowledgements

It has been said that the trials of life are unsupportable without the help of others. And so, we know that existence would be barren without others' help and courage to face struggles in life.

I thank all those who shared their spiritual journey with me and mentored me. You are my heroes for pointing to the answers to my many questions about what humans are and what I am.

A big thank you to Oprah Winfrey, Wayne Dyer, Deepak Chopra, Eckhart Tolle for their contributions to the world and the enrichment those contributions have brought to my life.

Also, deep gratitude to the healers who helped me on my way Dr. Trish Coughlin-Baitinger, Katherine Bohn, Matt Godwin, Sally Kingman, Lana McAra, Miriam Dow, Jonathan Cohen, Shari Landau, and Melinda Cahill.

More thanks, of course, to my parents always, and to my brothers and sisters who have been so devoted in their love for me. They are the pearls I wear around my neck.

To my children and grandchildren for all the love they give.

I thank my friends for their support to my evolution and development.

Most importantly, to my husband Dave, who always has my back.

Foreword

My original goal was to help women face the healing process in a beautiful way by first understanding what we are as human beings. However, upon reviewing the book, I saw that it applies equally to men. My second goal is to help us realize that we store information in our bodies, and we need to delete some of our thought patterns to grow and be happy and healthy within ourselves. I struggled myself with the idea of healing painful memories that were clearly in the way of my personal growth. I had created so many blocks put in place by my terrible fears that I needed to shed some light on them and on myself, to discover what was real and what was illusion.

Through meditation, mindfulness and other healing modalities, we can tear down the walls that block our evolutionary progress and move forward to the future we really desire. I developed the artistic drawing exercise of the roses to help us slow down and nurture the beauty we possess inside our hearts – to discover how glorious we are, with all our talents and gifts. My hope is that we can grow, heal and love more deeply and beautifully – both for ourselves and for others.

Introduction

You, Me, Us

Science dissects the external world in an effort to understand the language of our human ecosystem. The energy healer looks inward, finding the source of life and the connection to all that is within. Both seek truth and look at the same picture from different angles. Science has come to understand that this planet and the whole universe is made of energy, and those of us who are awake to it, know that energy follows intention and attention.

The problem is that we build our world with our unconscious thoughts so fast that we don't understand how the beginning creates the ending, or how our patterns of thought and emotion literally build our external world. Healing is simply slowing down to see our existence and what it means. When we slow down, we return to our essence and see how molecules of thoughts evolve into the bioplasma that creates our outer world.

Unprocessed trauma brings the illusion of darkness into our soul. We feel we are not enough and fill the "holes" with substitutes like discomfort and illness, addictive and obsessive behaviors. We forget we are divine and have unlimited access to The Golden Light of Healing. By bringing our attention back to our soul and its Source, we connect to the beauty and magnificence that is God in us and in everything around us.

We are the plasma that makes up the ocean and the stars. We are so much more than a human body, and when we accept trauma and negative thought patterns as our identity, we cut ourselves off from The Light that is the essence and nourishment of our souls. All that seems fractured is simply wholeness forgotten. As we remember, our souls expand into loving connection, and we gain the lives we never even knew we wanted.

Roses-Roses-Roses

Imagine that the circumstances and emotions of our lives are stored in our energetic and physical bodies as "roses" in all their colors. Each rose tells a story in all its glorious or ugly details. As you can see in the image I have illustrated, we are filled with roses containing "stories" we tell ourselves and "lessons" we have learned. For example, at the Thanksgiving table we might have "learned" that we are a good host, or that we are not good listeners, or that we haven't changed one bit since we were children. Another might be an anger we are letting go of, yet another might be a talent or dream that is coming to birth in us. Some are healthy roses, some are not. Some are out of date and expired and some are new and forming on a continuous stream of thought. The old rose patterns that are outdated must leave. Some drift away. Others need to be smoothed out of the biofield. Sometimes we need to listen to the story of the rose, and then choose to keep it or discard it.

There are many ways to release these patterns. In the following section, I will illustrate these with examples of healing from my personal experience. The first is illustrated on the left. On this particular day, I had aromatherapy massage along with a reiki healing. In a deep relaxed state of wonderment, I was enveloped by love. In the roses, I could see metaphorically what was actually happening inside my body as the healer was working on specific areas.

I saw the image of rose buds growing and blooming and leaving my body. The coming and going of the roses was a beautiful healing process. I could see rejuvenation coming into the areas that needed repair, and many layers of energy, each with its own color, frequency, and intelligence.

Part One – Open Heart

In the next four illustrations I am looking down on myself as though I were standing outside my body. My heart chakra area is very repressed, and my shoulders are pulling forward to protect my heart and feelings.

During the healing session, I am submerged in an ocean, and light is flying around. The Golden Light begins to encircle my heart.

My heart chakra begins to open and expand. I am filled with Golden Light and bliss. I experience relaxation within the strong ocean of love. The ache in my shoulder goes away. My heart is filled with aliveness and pulsating passion for life, with all its gifts and all its obstacles and sorrows. The root chakra is fortified and bursting with energy.

Energy is gently released from my throat chakra, dissolving blocks and making it possible for me to express my feelings more clearly.

The repressed heart chakra is released and gains vibrancy and splendor, aided by the healing energy of reiki, massage and aromatherapy.

True healing is not simply the healing of symptoms which appear in a physical body, it is healing of the whole self at all levels: physical, mental, emotional, and spiritual. Healing always requires our participation. In fact, self-healing is within our own power and is becoming more and more commonplace. This is our future.

Part Two – How Energy Works

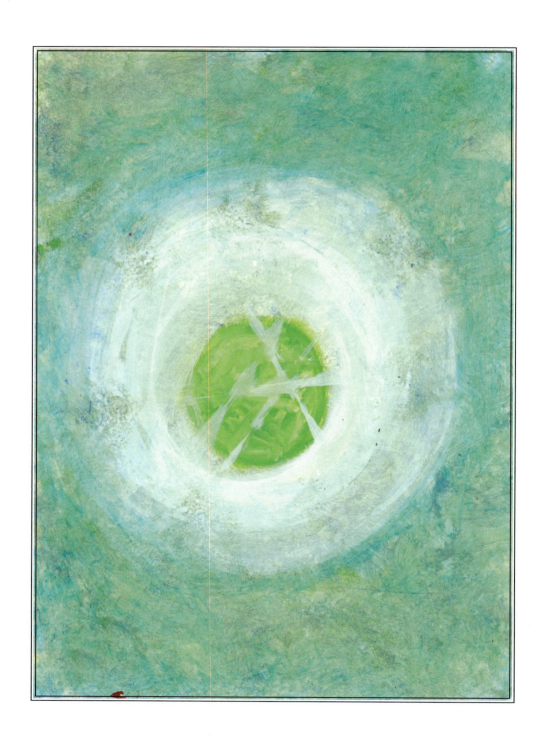

This simple illustration depicts a nucleus containing the potential for all things positive and negative. Our thoughts are creating the patterns -- like a foreign language that we don't know. Our body is a reflection of the energetic patterns present in each nucleus. The white lines in the center show how information moves throughout it.

This is you, your physical body. You are creating the building blocks of your life as each thought feeds information to the cells about how it should develop. The original thought may come from the self, from family inheritance, from the environment, or through cellular transfer. For example, if you are convinced that you are lucky, then luck will come to you. Your mind is a magnet.

Repetitive negative thoughts create a boomerang vibration that forms its own system within the body that affects our relationships with ourselves and with other people. For example, if you believe people are threatening to you, then you might be rude, which will bring out a similar reaction in them. If you recall that others are like you, you will treat them with respect, again calling forth a similar reaction.

Negative thought masses block the light lines that flow through our body. They also continue to attract more negative thoughts, growing from a thought seed to a thought-plant. These masses can become cancer or other forms of illness if they are not dissolved. Many things can help to dissolve them: energy healing, good conversation, massage, reiki, reflexology, psychotherapy, and so on… and you can do it yourself if you are conscious of your unhealthy emotions. In the illustration, the circular masses are releasing free radicals, producing chaos in the body.

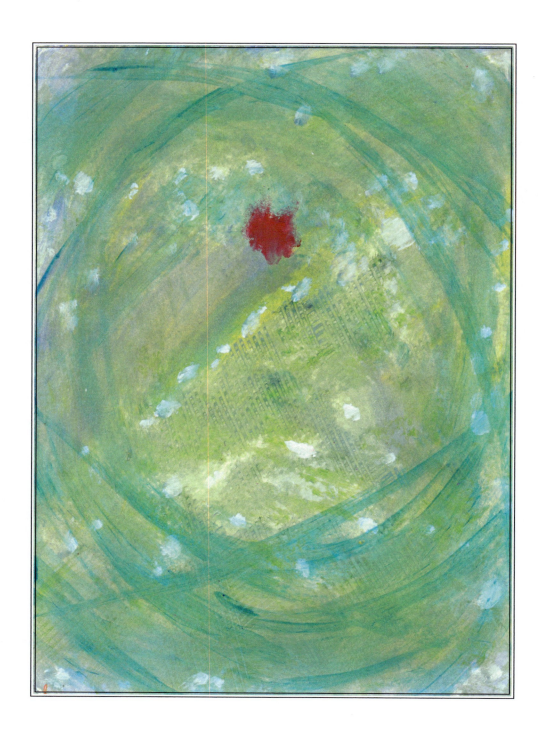

The red spot in this painting shows how a sparkling environment can be altered, blurred, and disrupted by pain and scarring from emotional trauma. This is the beginning of a thought becoming a physical pain.

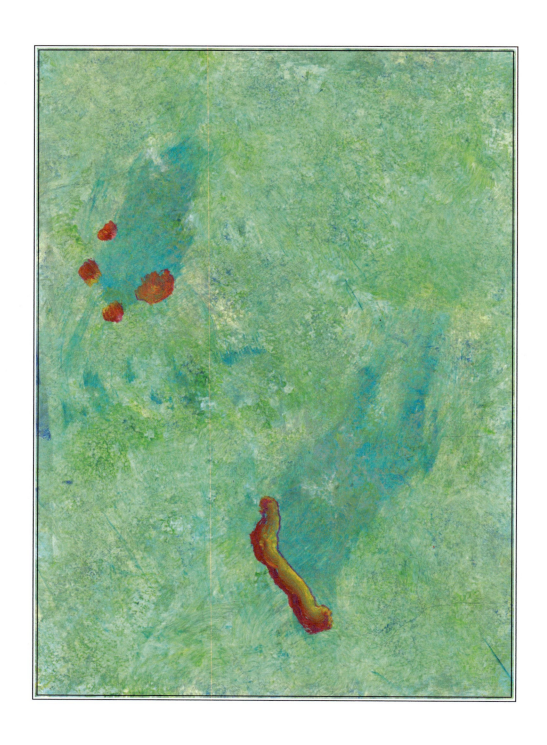

Here, we see a continued accumulation of negative energy in the original wounding from the last picture. The consciousness particles of wounding are increasing in number and will eventually cross the barrier from thought and energy to actual symptoms in the physical body.

Every thought has a vibration. Every vibration has a tone, even if inaudible. Each thought vibration impacts our physical body. The negative thought vibration is depicted here in red. As these red energies accumulate in a physical body, they create chaos. The physical body can no longer perform in balance and harmony.

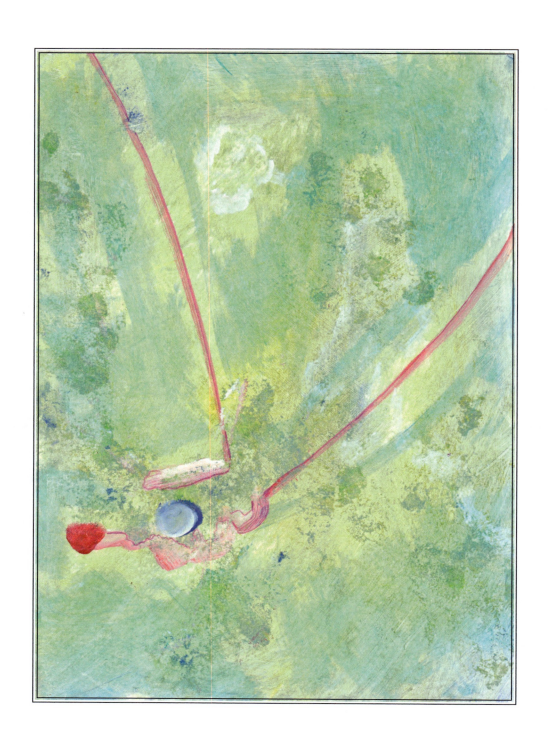

In this picture, the blue is the nucleus of discordant energy, the original belief. It acts like a magnet, attracting more and more energy and eventually manifesting itself as spiritual, emotional or physical conflict. And as long as it is fed, it will continue to grow and give off negative energy.

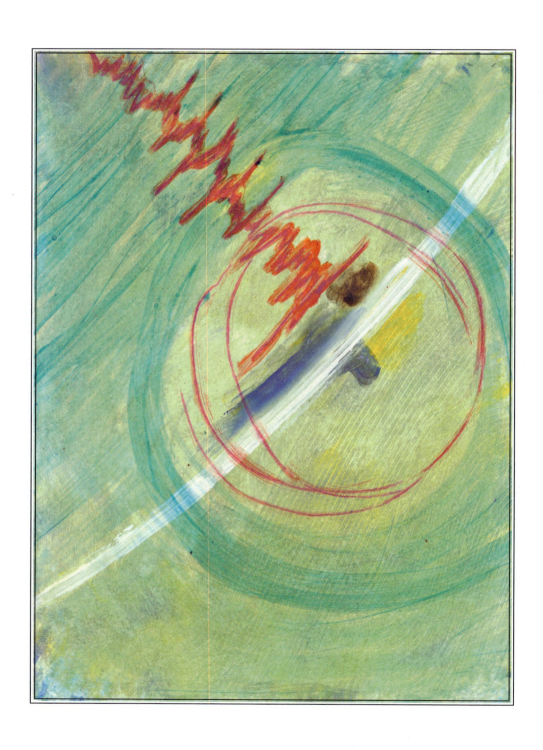

This is a picture of a recurrent pain located behind the shoulder. The red line is a deep electrical impulse coming from a pinched nerve and causing a feeling of fatigue in the heart region. Then the emotions of doubt, worry, sadness, and fear begin to take up residence in the same area. Here we see the entire heart and shoulder area throbbing with pain and fatigue. These are examples of patterns that can occur in this way in everybody.

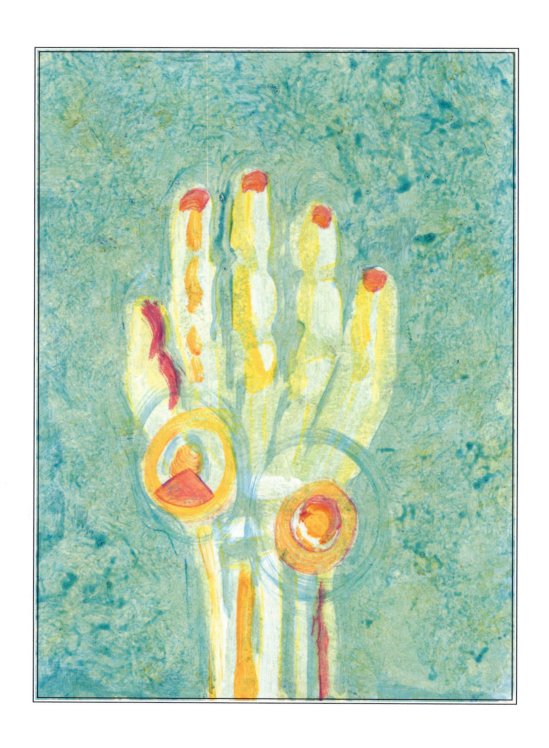

The red paint depicts a carpel-tunnel-like pain in the right hand of the artist. She created this condition by thinking the same thoughts again and again and again, and found relief through energy healing.

In this second example of physical discomfort created by thoughts and emotions, the red dot is at the heart point of reflexology. The physical, spiritual, and emotional pain in my heart center also created a pain at this point. The physical pain in my heart, I discovered, came from my wrestling with this world: Why is the world so full of war and injustice? It was a spiritual pain at the same time.

Part Three – Golden Light

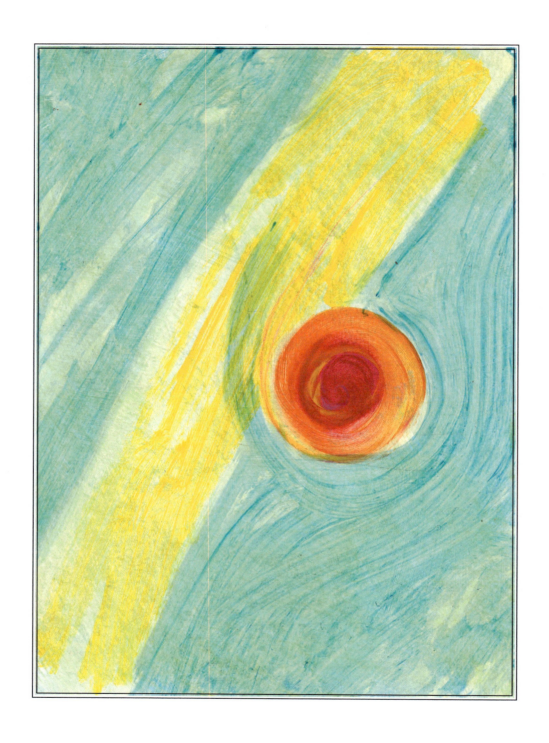

In the healing session, a Golden Vortex of light flows to the energy wound as both healer and client call for angelic help. What moves through the hands of the healer is really love. The angelic frequencies move through the crown chakra center down to the heart and through the arms and hands of the healer, transferring healing light from human to human as quantum beams of energy. Healing can come in many ways and through many kinds of people, trained or untrained. In every case, however, the healer is a transformer, connecting the angelic realms to clients, thus filtering the necessary information to the cells for change and healing.

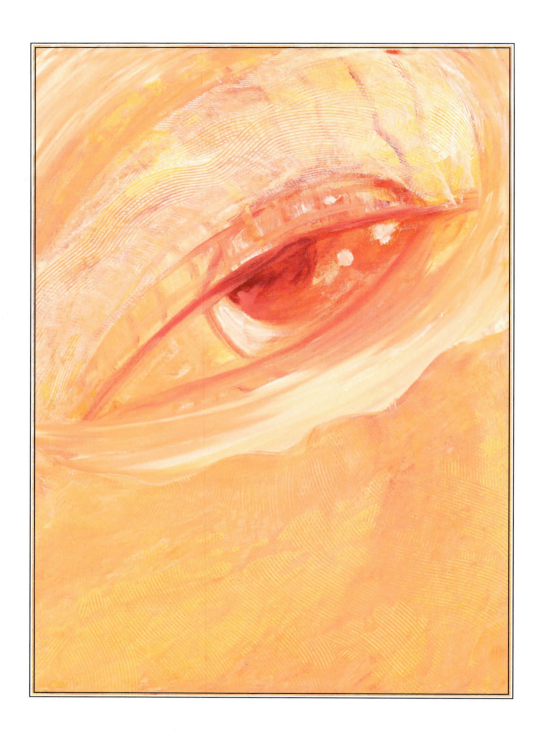

With the infusion of Golden Healing Light, the brilliant red burning vortex of pain, disharmony and imbalance begins to unravel. As the Light helps the body break out of habitual discomfort and remember its wholeness, the body returns to balance and heals itself.

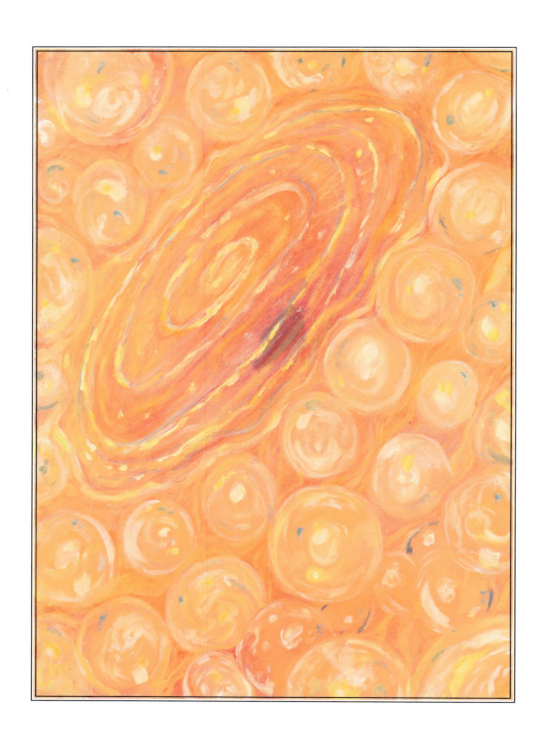

The Golden Light engulfs the negative energy, moving with intrinsic intelligence to neutralize the dis-ease in the shoulder.

Here we come down to the seed beneath the wound. It is a thought which has become a belief which has become a perception of the world. The prongs in this picture represent the vibration of conflict between what we have been taught and who we truly are. Like a tuning fork, each sends a seemingly opposing signal into the world. Healing dissolves and resolves these with the Golden Light of pure love and acceptance, restoring the natural flow of the energy.

The thoughts generated by the seed of conflict are swept away. The pain created by the habitual thoughts is also cleaned and cleared.

The body has returned to a healthy state, filled with light and ease of movement.

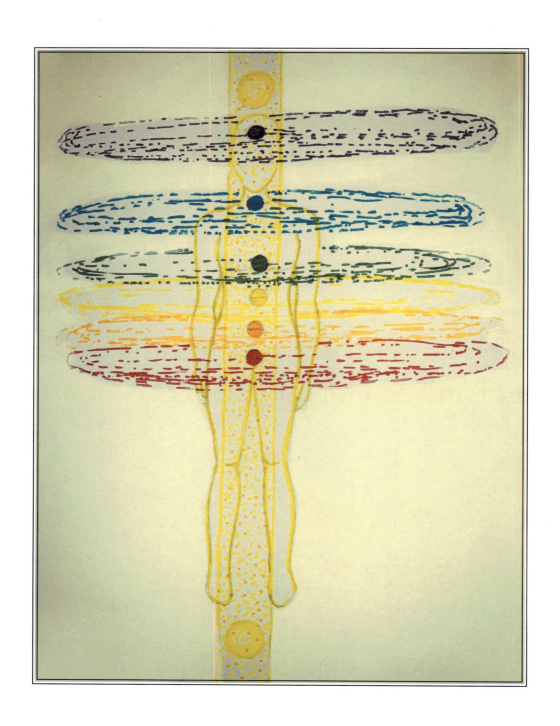

The gift of Golden Light comes down into the body through a channel shaped like a cylinder of energy. The illustration on the left is a modernized version of the traditional Hindu image of the chakras. When I experienced it myself, I saw living opalescent energy moving up and down the channel and through colorful circular disks, flat like CDs, and filled with information about the mind-body-spirit, each with its own beautiful musical accompaniment of chiming tones. The horizontal line on the disk is a point of balance.

The chakra colors and the opalescent light from the channel radiate in all directions.

Part Four – Creative Ways to Self-Nurture

Golden Light Meditation

Mindful relaxation and meditation nurture our mind, body, and spirit just as our physical bodies are nurtured by healthy food and movement. Many forms of mindfulness are possible to keep us in balance. Use the following meditation to call in the Golden Light of Healing while in a restful state.

I ask my spiritual guides to help me call in the golden healing light that will assist me in balancing and restoring my cells to perfect health. I am present to my own nurturing and wellness starting with healthy choices that my soul needs along with my body.

Coloring Pages

Color the roses while saying an affirmation with intention to clear away unwanted patterns. Build your own positive statements to infuse love into your inner self.

You will need a blank piece of paper, a pen, and colored pencils or markers.

You can also print this out larger on canvas paper and paint.

1. Place your name on the coloring paper.

2. Write as many affirmations as possible on the blank paper.

3. I Am + positive self-statements (list talents.)

4. I Am working towards (personal goals)

5. I Am now letting go of (sadness, anger, frustration, etc.)

6. Color a rose while repeating softly your affirmation and feel love for yourself

7. See next page for more sample affirmations.

Affirmations

I am always learning–clearing–growing.

I am healthy and whole.

I honor my name.

I am present and aware.

I am working on my blocks and personal issues in order to clear the house of my spirit and soul.

I love myself, spirit and soul.

My challenges have been for my soul's learning, and I am clearing out thoughts that are out of date.

I am working on new goals daily.

I am talented in many areas.

Gratefulness is my heart's peace of mind.

I receive blessings and give blessings.

I am loved.

Note to Self

May I be open to the healing love present in this work, for my
greatest good and highest purpose. (Sally Kingman)

1.

2.

3.

4.

5.

6.

7.

Recommended Resources

There are many helpful resources for healing. These are some of the ones that have been most helpful to me:

Greg Braden – *Divine Matrix*

Bruce Lipton – *Biology of Belief*

Alex Grey – *The Mission of Art*

Barbara Brennan – *Light Emerging, Hands of Light, Core Light Healing*

Deepak Chopra – *How to Know God, Perfect Health*

Eckhart Tolle – *The New Earth*

Louise Hay – *You Can Heal Your Life*

Carolyn Myss – *Energy Anatomy, Why People Don't Heal and How They Can*

The Mindful Movement Healing Meditation, YouTube

Deepak Chopra – Chakra Balancing Meditation 1 -2-3, YouTube

Golden Light Meditation with James Van Praagh, YouTube

Regina Madsen

Regina has always focused on the positive, seeing the beauty in human beings and their creations in architecture, engineering, and art. Facing the evidence that human life also contains suffering has stimulated in her a desire to heal. Her early years as a high-end hairdresser brought her a wealth of human experience and developed a compassionate ear for others. In this way she developed an interest in the esoteric aspects of life, which she pursued through self-study and many classes in a variety of healing modalities. She is now a reiki practitioner, having completed Usui Reiki Level III Master Training.

In addition to her interest in the healing arts, for over two decades Regina has worked in the decorative arts field, both commercial and residential, doing projects from large scale murals to faux painting. Among the many companies she has worked for are InterArch Architecture firm, Childs Dreyfus, Elle Design, and Gray Mare Interiors. She was interviewed for her fifty-foot mural of "Passage of Time" in *Chester Life Magazine* and has had her artwork featured in *Home* Magazine and *New Vision*. She has also done many artistic projects for charity, including a large-scale ocean–themed mural in the Children's Crisis Center in Philadelphia, a mural donated to Habitat for Humanity called "Helping Hands," and a mural donated to Kennedy Water Keepers, called "Noah."

Printed in the United States
By Bookmasters